Oceans of the World

Southern Ocean

Louise and Richard Spilsbury

a Capstone company — publishers for children

Raintree is an imprint of Capstone Global Library Limited, a company incorporated in England and Wales having its registered office at 7 Pilgrim Street, London, EC4V 6LB – Registered company number: 6695582

www.raintree.co.uk
myorders@raintree.co.uk

Edited by Penny West
Designed by Steve Mead
Original illustrations © Capstone Global Library Ltd 2015
Picture research by Tracy Cummins
Production by Victoria Fitzgerald
Originated by Capstone Global Library Ltd
Printed and bound in China by Leo Paper Group

ISBN 978 1 406 28753 0
18 17 16 15 14
10 9 8 7 6 5 4 3 2 1

British Library Cataloguing in Publication Data
A full catalogue record for this book is available from the British Library.

Spilsbury, Louise and Richard
Southern Ocean. – (Oceans of the World)

Acknowledgements
We would like to thank the following for permission to reproduce photographs: Corbis: Momatiuk - Eastcott, 25; Getty Images: Danita Delimont, 21, Michael S. Nolan, 23, Mike Hill, 13, Ralph Lee Hopkins, 12, Sue Flood, 27, Ty Milford, 26; Science Source: Hubertus Kanus, 20; Shutterstock: AndreAnita, 11, Anton Ivanov, 16, AridOcean, 7, 10, axily, 9, Cover Bottom, leonello calvetti, Cover Middle, Lisa Strachan, 4, Matt Berger, Cover Top, Mogens Trolle, 18, steve estvanik, 22, VolodymyrGoinyk, 15, Zmiter, Design Element; SuperStock: Biosphoto, 14, Minden Pictures, 17, 24, NHPA, 6; Thinkstock: ChristianWilkinsoni, 19.

We would like to thank Michael Bright for his invaluable help in the preparation of this book.

Contents

Some words are shown in bold, **like this**. You can find out what they mean by looking in the glossary.

About the Southern Ocean

The Southern Ocean, also known as the Antarctic Ocean, is one of the five oceans of the world. An ocean is a vast area of salty water. The world's oceans are connected. Together they cover almost three-quarters of our planet.

The Southern Ocean is the fourth largest of the world's five oceans.

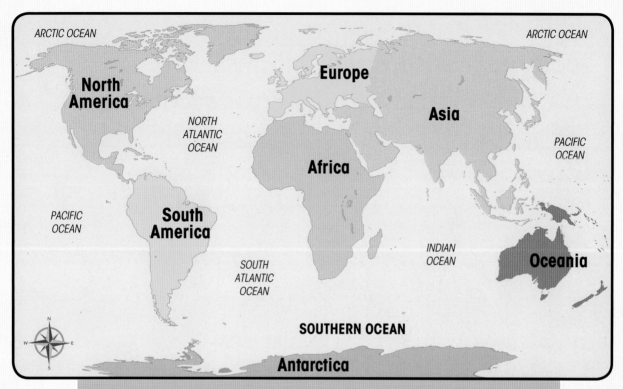

ARCTIC OCEAN

ARCTIC OCEAN

North
America

Europe

Asia

NORTH
ATLANTIC
OCEAN

PACIFIC
OCEAN

Africa

PACIFIC
OCEAN

South
America

INDIAN
OCEAN

Oceania

SOUTH
ATLANTIC
OCEAN

SOUTHERN OCEAN

Antarctica

The narrowest part of the Southern Ocean is between the tip of South America and Antarctica.

The Southern Ocean is the ring of ocean that circles round Antarctica. Antarctica is the Earth's fifth largest **continent**. The northern edge of the Southern Ocean merges into the Atlantic, Indian and Pacific Oceans.

The other four oceans are mostly divided up by the **continents**. The Southern Ocean is different. It mainly runs into the other oceans. It was named a separate ocean in 2000 because its water is much colder than the water of the oceans it joins.

The icy waters of the Southern Ocean meet the waters of the Pacific Ocean.

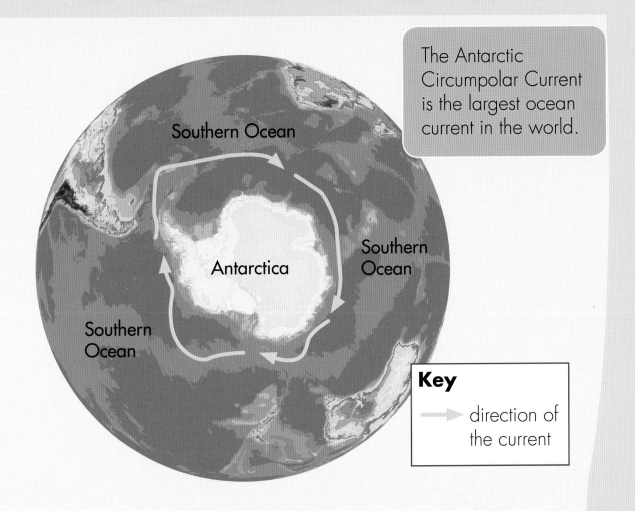

Southern Ocean

Southern Ocean

Antarctica

Southern Ocean

The Antarctic Circumpolar Current is the largest ocean current in the world.

Key

→ direction of the current

There is a strong **current** of very cold water that goes round and round the edge of the Southern Ocean. This is called the Antarctic Circumpolar Current. It keeps all of the water in the Southern Ocean cold, even where it meets other oceans.

Geography

The Southern Ocean is very deep. At the bottom of the ocean there are dips called **basins** that are shaped like bowls. There are hills with flat tops called **plateaus**. There are also deep, narrow **trenches**, such as the South Sandwich Trench.

Southern Ocean fact file	
Total area:	20,327,000 million square kilometres (5,926,400 square miles)
Average depth:	4 to 5 kilometres (2.5 to 3 miles)
Lowest point:	7,235 metres (23,736 feet) below sea level at the southern end of the South Sandwich Trench
Length of coastline (Antarctica):	17,968 kilometres (11,164 miles)

The water over the Antarctic continental shelf is 400 to 800 metres (1,300 to 2,600 feet) deep. The world average is 60 metres (200 feet).

The land at the edge of Antarctica that lies under the ocean is called a **continental shelf**. The water above this shelf is a bit shallower than the rest of the ocean, but it is still deeper than the average depth of water above other continental shelves.

Seas are smaller areas of an ocean found near the coast and usually partly surrounded by land. There are several seas in the Southern Ocean, such as the Weddell Sea. The Weddell Sea is huge. At its widest point, the Weddell Sea is over 2,000 kilometres (1,242 miles) across!

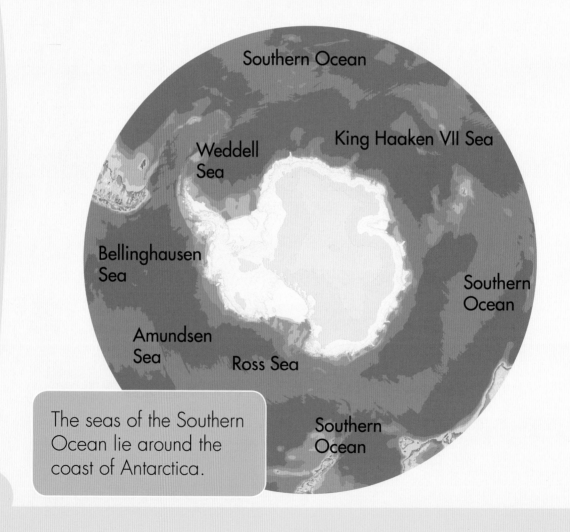

Southern Ocean

King Haaken VII Sea

Weddell Sea

Bellinghausen Sea

Southern Ocean

Amundsen Sea

Ross Sea

Southern Ocean

The seas of the Southern Ocean lie around the coast of Antarctica.

Over a third of the world's Adelie penguins live in the Ross Sea.

The Ross Sea is a remote and rarely visited part of the world. There are animals here that are found nowhere else, such as the Ross Sea killer whale and the Colossal squid. This rarely seen squid is 13 metres (43 feet) long and has eyes bigger than dinner plates!

Weather

The Antarctic region is the coldest place on Earth. It is covered in ice up to 2.25 kilometres (1.4 miles) thick. In winter (June to September) it is freezing cold over the Southern Ocean. In summer it's still very cold, but it's light almost all day and night.

For a short time in winter, parts of the Southern Ocean are dark almost 24 hours a day.

Strong winds over the Southern Ocean cause rough waves during much of the year.

The Southern Ocean is affected by the strongest winds on the planet. Winds nearby often blow at more than 120 kilometres (75 miles) per hour. Sometimes they reach speeds of up to 250 kilometres (155 miles) per hour. These winds can cause dangerous waves.

Sea ice

In winter, when it gets colder, the Southern Ocean around the edges of Antarctica freezes. The ice covers a large part of the ocean and is over a metre (3 feet) thick. By summer, this sea ice has melted and most of the Southern Ocean is free of ice.

September is when the biggest area of the Southern Ocean is frozen.

Icebergs are as hard as rock and can break a deadly hole in the side of any boat that runs into them.

Icebergs are big blocks of floating ice. Many icebergs in the Southern Ocean come from the **ice shelves** around the Antarctic. Ice shelves are thick floating platforms of ice that form where ice flows down to the coast and floats on the water without breaking away.

Islands

There are lots of islands in the Southern Ocean. Some are just lumps of rocks jutting out of the water. Others are hundreds of kilometres long and have high, rugged mountains. Most of the islands are covered in ice.

Half Moon Island is one of the South Shetland Islands. Lots of chinstrap penguins have their young here.

Ross Island has four volcanoes. Mount Erebus is the only one active.

Some of the islands are named after the explorers who discovered different parts of the Antarctic region in the past. For example, Ross Island was discovered by the British explorer Sir James Clark Ross in 1841.

Animals

The Southern Ocean is home to millions of birds, seals, whales and other animals. Leopard seals have a thick layer of fat called **blubber** to keep them warm in cold water. They hunt other seals, fish and penguins. They often catch penguins as the birds jump off the ice into the water.

The leopard seal got its name because its coat is spotted, rather like a leopard's.

The wandering albatross has wings that reach up to 3.4 metres (11 feet) across!

Wandering albatrosses spend most of their lives gliding above the Southern Ocean. They feed on fish and squid from the ocean and rest on the surface of the water. These huge birds visit islands in the ocean to have their young.

People

It is too cold to live in most places around the Southern Ocean, but people live and work in sub-Antarctic islands, Antarctic bases and **research stations**. At research stations, scientists study things such as the weather, ice and wildlife in the Antarctic region.

Mawson Research Station has bedrooms, a dining room, a kitchen, a library and sitting rooms for scientists to relax in.

Weddell Sea

Mawson Research Station

Ross Sea

It can take two days to unload all the supplies from a ship to a research station.

Ships and aircraft bring important supplies across the Southern Ocean to the research stations. They bring food, scientific equipment, vehicles, spare parts for machinery, and fuel to power the machinery.

Tourists come by boat and by air across the Southern Ocean to see the ocean wildlife, the icebergs and the coast of Antarctica. Sometimes they travel in big ships called icebreakers that can cut through the sea ice.

Antarctic cruise ships often stop to show tourists cute Gentoo penguins like these.

Humpback whales come to the surface to breathe in oxygen.

Every year more tourists come to the region. Some experts are worried that more visitors could disturb the wildlife. Whales feed here in summer then travel to warmer waters to have their young. If whales are disturbed and leave their feeding grounds too soon, they might not survive the trip.

Resources

One of the most important resources in the Southern Ocean is krill. People catch millions of these tiny sea creatures. They use krill to make food for animals and oil for human health products.

The amount of krill in the Southern Ocean could cover Australia around four and a half times!

Many **baleen whales** in the Southern Ocean depend on krill.

Animals such as fish, seals, penguins and whales rely on krill for food. That is why there are rules about how many krill the fishing boats can catch. The rules make sure there are enough krill left for whales and other animals to eat.

25

Famous places

Most people who visit Antarctica by boat travel through Drake Passage. Drake Passage is a fairly narrow stretch of the Southern Ocean between Antarctica and South America.

Drake Passage is a dangerous stretch of water known for bad weather, giant waves, strong winds and icebergs!

Weddell Sea

Ross Sea

● Ross Ice Shelf

The Ross Ice Shelf lies at the top of the Ross Sea and in some places where it meets the water it is up to 60 meters (200 feet) high.

Another famous place is the Ross Ice Shelf. This is the largest body of floating ice in the world. Most scientific teams that have explored Antarctica have crossed this sea ice.

Fun facts

- Antarctica holds about 90 per cent of all the ice on the planet, and as this ice melts it increases the amount of water in the oceans.

- The Antarctic Circumpolar Current is 21,000 kilometres (13,048 miles) long and it moves eastwards all the time. It carries 100 times the flow of all the world's rivers put together!

- The world's lowest air temperature ever recorded was −89.2 degrees Celsius (−128.6 degrees Fahrenheit) at Vostok **research station**, near the **South Pole**, in July 1983.

- There is around 350 million tonnes (386 million tons) of krill in the Southern Ocean. This sounds like a lot but **baleen whales** alone eat 30–50 million tonnes (33–55 tons) of krill in the Antarctic each year.

Quiz

1 Which **continent** does the Southern Ocean surround?

2 What is the Antarctic Circumpolar Current?

3 Where are the strongest winds on the planet?

4 What are krill?

Answers

1 The Southern Ocean surrounds Antarctica.

2 The Antarctic Circumpolar Current is a strong **current** of very cold water that goes round the edge of the Southern Ocean.

3 Over the Southern Ocean.

4 Krill are tiny sea creatures people use to make food for animals and oil for human health products.

Glossary

baleen whale whale that feeds on krill by filtering them out of water using huge plates of bone in their mouth called baleen

basin large, bowl-shaped dip in the Earth's surface

blubber thick layer of fat under an animal's skin

continent one of seven huge areas of land on Earth

continental shelf part of a continent that is underwater and slopes down to the ocean floor

current body of water moving in one direction

ice shelf thick slab of ice attached to the coastline

plateau hill or area of raised ground with a flat or level top

research station place built for scientists to research and study in

sea smaller area of an ocean usually found near the land and usually partly surrounded by land

South Pole southernmost point on Earth

trench long, narrow and deep hole in the ground

Find out more

Books
Deep Oceans (Earth's Last Frontiers), Ellen Labrecque
  (Raintree, 2014)
Introducing Antarctica (Introducing Continents), Anita Ganeri
  (Raintree, 2014)
Ocean (Eyewitness), Miranda MacQuitty (Dorling Kindersley,
  2014)

Websites
Learn more about the Southern Ocean, Antarctica and its
wildlife at
www.bbc.co.uk/nature/ecozones/Antarctic_ecozone

Learn about threats to oceans and coasts at
**wwf.panda.org/about_our_earth/blue_planet/
problems**

Index